Life Story of a
Ladybug

Charlotte Guillain

Heinemann
LIBRARY

Chicago, Illinois

Edited by Catherine Veitch and Gina Kammer
Designed by Richard Parker and Peggie Carley
Picture research by Mica Brancic
Production by Victoria Fitzgerald
Originated by Capstone Global Library Ltd

Library of Congress Cataloging-in-Publication Data
Cataloging-in-publication information is on file with the Library of Congress.
ISBN 978-1-4846-0488-5 (hardcover)
ISBN 978-1-4846-0493-9 (paperback)
ISBN 978-1-4846-0503-5 (eBook PDF)

Acknowledgments
We would like to thank the following for permission to reproduce photographs:
Ardea: Steve Hopkin, 20; FLPA: Gary K. Smith, 7, Matt Cole, 5, 21, Nigel Cattlin, 17, Phil McLean, 26; Nature Picture Library: Nature Production, 10; Photoshot: Jean-Claude Carton, 23; Science Source: E. R. Degginger, 16, Explorer, 25, Harry Rogers, 8, 28 (left), Mark Bowler, 18, Perennou Nuridsany, 9; Shutterstock: AlexussK (stone design element), cover and throughout, Christian Musat, 12, D. Kucharski and K. Kucharska, 11, 28 (right), Erik Mandre, 6, jannoon028 (grass border), throughout, ninii, cover, Pakhnyushcha, 19, Photo Fun, 13, Risto0, 27, Yellowj, 4, 29 (bottom), Yuliya Proskurina (green leaves border), cover and throughout; SuperStock: Biosphoto, 14, 15, 29 (top), 24, Juniors, 22

We would like to thank Michael Bright for his assistance in the preparation of this book.

Every effort has been made to contact copyright holders of material reproduced in this book. Any omissions will be rectified in subsequent printings if notice is given to the publisher.

All the Internet addresses (URLs) given in this book were valid at the time of going to press. However, due to the dynamic nature of the Internet, some addresses may have changed, or sites may have changed or ceased to exist since publication. While the author and publisher regret any inconvenience this may cause readers, no responsibility for any such changes can be accepted by either the author or the publisher.

Contents

Some words are shown in bold, **like this**. You can find out what they mean by looking in the glossary.

What is a Ladybug?

A ladybug is a type of animal called an **insect**. Insects are animals with three pairs of legs and a body with three main parts. Many insects have wings.

Most ladybugs are less than half an inch long. They usually have red or yellow covers over their wings with a spotted pattern.

A Ladybug's Life Story

Like all animals, a ladybug goes through different stages as it grows into an adult. These stages make up an animal's life story.

adult

young

young

adult

Follow the life story of ladybugs and watch them change in unusual ways as they develop and grow.

It Starts with an Egg

A ladybug starts its life as an egg. The egg is tiny, smooth, and oval shaped. Some ladybug eggs are a yellow color.

A female ladybug lays her eggs under a leaf. The eggs are safe there from rain and from **predators** that might eat them.

The Egg Hatches

A ladybug **larva** hatches out of its egg after four to ten days.

Some ladybug larvae are gray and black with several body **segments.** Other ladybug larvae are brown or yellow.

A Growing Larva

A ladybug larva eats small bugs, such as **aphids** or mites. It keeps eating and gets bigger and bigger.

A larva's skin splits four times as it grows bigger. Each time its skin splits, the larva crawls out with a new skin.

Changing into a Pupa

After three to six weeks, the ladybug larva attaches itself to a leaf. Then it becomes a **pupa**.

A pupa stays still on the leaf for about two weeks. It is changing into an adult ladybug. This change of body shape is called **metamorphosis.**

Changing into an Adult

When the pupa has changed into an adult ladybug, the skin splits open. An adult ladybug crawls out.

After a few hours, the ladybug's wing cases become a brighter color and spots appear. The wing cases also become harder and dry out. Then the ladybug is ready to fly.

Like all insects, an adult ladybug has a pair of **antennae** on its head. The ladybug uses its antennae to smell, taste, and feel.

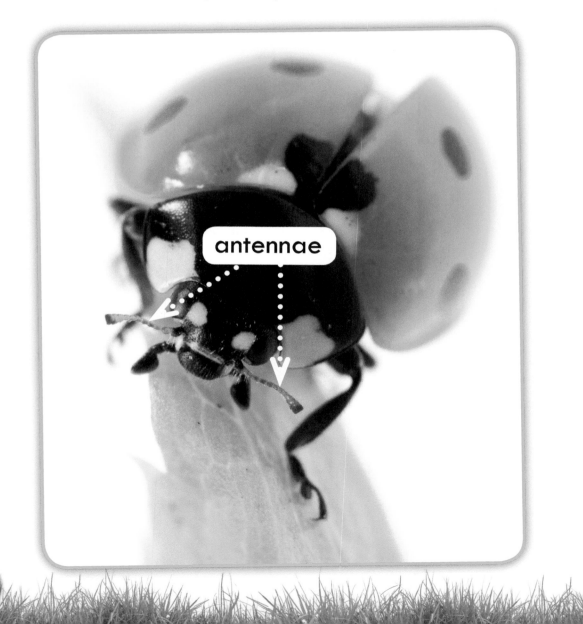

antennae

elytra

wings

The ladybug's wings are protected under spotted wing cases. These cases are called **elytra**.

A ladybug's bright color is a warning to predators. The color tells predators that it tastes bad. A ladybug also makes a sticky substance when a predator attacks.

An adult ladybug mainly eats aphids. If there aren't enough aphids, then the ladybug might eat other ladybugs' larvae or eggs.

Mating

A ladybug looks for a mate so they can continue the life story. Together they can **reproduce** and create new ladybugs.

A male and female ladybug have to find
each other to mate. They release a special
smell when they are ready to find a mate.

After mating the female ladybug lays eggs on a plant leaf. She chooses a plant that is eaten by bugs so that the larvae will have bugs to eat when they hatch.

A female ladybug usually lays eggs in spring when plants are growing. After laying the eggs, it leaves.

A Ladybug's Life

Some ladybugs only live for a few months. Other ladybugs can live for about a year. Some ladybugs stay somewhere sheltered through the cold winter months.

Some animals and birds eat ladybugs.
When a ladybug dies, the ladybug life
story is continued by its young.

Ladybug Life Story Diagram

eggs

larva

pupa

adult ladybug

Glossary

antennae long, thin feelers on an insect's head that it uses to feel and smell

aphid insect that sucks the juices of plants

elytra tough cases over a ladybug's delicate wings

insect type of animal with no backbone that has three main body parts and three pairs of legs

larva stage in an animal's life before it becomes an adult

metamorphosis stages where an animal changes body shape and appearance

predator animal that hunts and eats other animals

pupa the stage of an insect's life when it changes from a larva to an adult

reproduce to lay eggs or give birth to young

segment separate section

Find Out More

Books

Ask a Bug
   (Dorling Kindersley, 2011)

Insects Sticker Book, Anthony Wootton
   (Usborne, 2010)

Websites

http://www.bbc.co.uk/nature/life/Coccinellidae
Visit the BBC Nature website to find out more about ladybugs and watch video clips.

**http://www.arkive.org/seven-spot-ladybird/
coccinella-septempunctata/image-A8736.html**
The Arkive website has plenty of information and photos of the different stages of a ladybug's life.

Index